CONNECT BIBLE STUDIES

G000019255

The Simpsons

Matt Groening
(Twentieth Century Fox)

Homer
Marge
Bart
Lisa

www.connectbiblestudies.com

connect

linking the Word to the world

CONNECT BIBLE STUDIES: The Simpsons

Published in this format by Scripture Union, 207-209 Queensway, Bletchley, MK2 2EB, England.

Scripture Union is an international Christian charity working with churches in more than 130 countries providing resources to bring the good news about Jesus Christ to children, young people and families — and to encourage them to develop spiritually through the Bible and prayer.

As well as a network of volunteers, staff and associates who run holidays, church-based events and school Christian groups, Scripture Union produces a wide range of publications and supports those who use the resources through training programmes.

Email: info@scriptureunion.org.uk
Internet: www.scriptureunion.org.uk

Damaris Trust enables people to relate Christian faith and contemporary culture. It helps them to think about the issues within society from a Christian perspective and to explore God's truth as it is revealed in the Bible. Damaris provides resources via the Internet, workshops, publications and products.

Email: office@damaris.org
Internet: www.damaris.org

ALSO AVAILABLE AS AN ELECTRONIC DOWNLOAD: www.connectbiblestudies.com

Chief editor: Nick Pollard
Consultant Editor: Andrew Clark
Managing Editor: Di Archer
Written by Di Archer, James Murkett, Caroline Puntis, Tony Watkins

First published 2001
ISBN 1 85999 529 2

British Library Cataloguing-in-Publication Data: a catalogue record for this book is available from the British Library.

Cover design and print production by:
CPO, Garcia Estate, Canterbury Road, Worthing, West Sussex BN13 1BW.

Other titles in this series:

Harry Potter and the Goblet of Fire ISBN 1 85999 578 0
The Matrix ISBN 1 85999 579 9
U2: All that you can't leave behind ISBN 1 85999 580 2
Billy Elliot ISBN 1 85999 581 0
Chocolat ISBN 1 85999 608 6
Game Shows ISBN 1 85999 609 4
How to be Good ISBN 1 85999 610 8
Destiny's Child: Survivor ISBN 1 85999 613 2
AI (Artificial Intelligence) ISBN 1 85999 626 4
The Lord of the Rings ISBN 1 85999 634 5

And more titles following — check www.connectbiblestudies.com for latest titles or ask at any good Christian bookshop.

connect

linking the Word to the world

Using Connect Bible Studies

What Are These Studies?

These innovative home group Bible studies have two aims. Firstly, we design them to enable group members to dig into their Bibles and get to know them better. Secondly, we aim to help members to think through topical issues in a Biblical way. Hence the studies are based on a current popular book or film etc. The issues raised by these are the subjects for the Bible studies.

We do not envisage that all members will always be able to watch the films or read the books, or indeed that they will always want to. A summary is always provided. However, our vision is that knowing about these films and books empowers Christians to engage with friends and colleagues about them. Addressing issues from a Biblical perspective gives Christians confidence that they know what they think, and can bring a distinctive angle to bear in conversations.

The studies are produced in sets of four — i.e. four weeks' worth of group Bible Study material. These are available in print published by Scripture Union from your local Christian bookshop, or via the Internet at www.connectbiblestudies.com. Anyone can sign up for a free monthly email newsletter that announces the new studies and provides other information (sign up on the Connect Bible Studies website at www.connectbiblestudies.com/uk/register).

How Do I Use Them?

We design the studies to stimulate creative thought and discussion within a Biblical context. Each section therefore has a range of questions or options from which you as leader may choose in order to tailor the study to your group's needs and desires. Different approaches may appeal at different times, so the studies aim to supply lots of choice. Whilst adhering to the main aim of corporate Bible study, some types of questions may enable this for your group better than others — so take your pick.

Group members should be supplied with the appropriate sheet that they can fill in, each one also showing the relevant summary.

Leader's notes contain:

1. Opening Questions

These help your group settle in to discussion, whilst introducing the topics. They may be straightforward, personal or creative, but are aiming to provoke a response.

2. Summary

We suggest the summary of the book or film will follow now, read aloud if necessary. There may well be reactions that group members want to express even before getting on to the week's issue.

3. Key Issue

Again, either read from the leader's notes, or summarised.

4. Bible Study

Lots of choice here. Choose as appropriate to suit your group — get digging into the Bible. Background reading and texts for further help and study are suggested, but please use the material provided to inspire your group to explore their Bibles as much as possible. A concordance might be a handy standby for looking things up. A commentary could be useful too, such as the *New Bible Commentary 21st Century Edition* (IVP, 1994). The idea is to help people to engage with the truth of God's word, wrestling with it if necessary but making it their own.

Don't plan to work through every question here. Within each section the two questions explore roughly the same ground but from different angles or in different ways. Our advice is to take one question from each section. The questions are open-ended so each ought to yield good discussion — though of course any discussion in a Bible study may need prompting to go a little further.

5. Implications

Here the aim is to tie together the perspectives gained through Bible study and the impact of the book or film. The implications may be personal, a change in worldview, or new ideas for relating to non-churchgoers. Choose questions that adapt to the flow of the discussion.

6. Prayer

Leave time for it! We suggest a time of open prayer, or praying in pairs if the group would prefer. Encourage your members to focus on issues from your study that had a particular impact on them. Try different approaches to prayer — light a candle, say a prayer each, write prayers down, play quiet worship music — aim to facilitate everyone to relate to God.

7. Background Reading

You will find links to some background reading on the Connect Bible Studies website: www.connectbiblestudies.com/

8. Online Discussion

You can discuss the studies online with others on the Connect Bible Studies website at www.connectbiblestudies.com/discuss/

Scriptures referred to are taken from the Holy Bible, New International Version (NIV). Copyright © 1973, 1978, 1984 by International Bible Society. Other Bible translations can, of course, be used for the studies and having a range of translations in a group can be helpful and useful in discussion.

www.connectbiblestudies.com

connect
linking the Word to the world

The Simpsons

Matt Groening (20th Century Fox)

Part One: Homer

'Dad, you must really love us to sink so low.'
Bart to Homer

Please read Using Connect Bible Studies *before leading a Bible study using this material.*

Opening Questions

Choose one of these questions.

Are you a fan of *The Simpsons*? Why or why not?	What is your favourite doughnut? How many can you eat in one sitting?
To what extent is Homer a fair representation of Western men?	In what ways are you like Homer?

Summary

Homer J Simpson is the 'father-figure' in the Simpson household. He spends his days working as a safety inspector at Springfield Nuclear Power Plant where his laziness is all too visible. However, when a situation develops at the plant he manages to save it from meltdown — admittedly by guesswork.

Homer's hobbies include eating doughnuts and other fatty foods, sitting in Moe's Tavern drinking Duff beer, ten-pin bowling and baiting Ned Flanders (the Christian next door). Despite his obsession with all things culinary, Homer is a man who cares deeply for his family. His devotion to Marge is unquestionable — he even resists the temptation to have an affair with lovely Country and Western singer Lurleen Lumpkin. His love for his children — though not always clearly expressed — is evident. He is prepared to pursue various schemes to provide for their needs and wants. He tries to give them good advice when it is necessary.

Catchphrases that Homer uses include 'D'oh!' when he is upset (frequently) and 'Mmm ...' when he is tempted (even more frequently!). He has a mild disregard for the law — for a brief time he was the 'Beer Baron', producing illegal liquor during Springfield's prohibition. Homer's character underpins the whole family, and he is arguably the most important personality in the whole show.

Key Issue: Homer

Think Homer — think doughnuts and beer. Is this all there is to the TV-addicted dad who leads his family to the couch with persistent determination? Yet he loves his family, provides for them and approaches others with generosity. Does the Bible affirm these characteristics? What of his doughnut obsession? Does the Bible turn a blind eye to this? If Homer is being set up as a typical male, what of his attitude towards spirituality? Do his homemade attempts at religion ring true with what the Bible says?

Bible Study

Choose one question from each section.

1. Role — provider

'I'll work from midnight to eight, come home, sleep for five minutes, eat breakfast, sleep six more minutes, shower, then I have ten minutes to bask in Lisa's love, then I'm off to the power plant fresh as a daisy.' (Homer)

♦   Read Ruth 2:1, 2, 17–3:18; 4:9–15. Why did Naomi consider Boaz to be a suitable husband for Ruth? How did he provide for her and Naomi?

Leaders: A kinsman-redeemer acted to protect and provide for members of his extended family who needed help. This included buying back land that a poor relative had been forced to sell, rescuing a relative from slavery, or taking responsibility to provide an heir for a brother who had died. See Deuteronomy 25:5-10.

♦   Read 1 Timothy 5:1–8. Why is providing for our nearest and dearest 'putting our religion into practice'? How should we treat those outside our immediate family? Why is negligence in these matters condemned as denying our faith?

Leaders: Widows had no state support at all, so were especially vulnerable.

2. Strength — big-hearted man

'You deserve all the finest things in the world and although I can give them to you, they will be repossessed and I will be hunted down like a dog.' (Homer to Marge)

♦ Read Exodus 32:1, 7–14. How did Moses argue for the Israelites to be spared? In what way was this 'big-hearted' of him?

♦ Read 1 Thessalonians 2:1–20. How did Paul, Silas and Timothy demonstrate love for the Thessalonians? What impact did it have on the people?

3. Weakness — gluttony

'Two-hundred-thirty-nine pounds?! I'm a blimp! Why are all the good things so tasty?' (Homer upon weighing himself)

♦ Read Proverbs 23:17–25. Why is gluttony condemned? How can it be avoided?

♦ Read Isaiah 22:8b–14. Why were the inhabitants of Jerusalem condemned for eating and drinking? What attitudes should they have shown — to God and in their particular situation?

Leaders: Isaiah is denouncing the people of Jerusalem because of their attitude when the city was besieged — probably by the Babylonians under Nebuchadnezzar during the reign of Hezekiah.

4. Spiritual outlook — self-justification

'I want to share something with you — the three little sentences that will get you through life. Number one: "Cover for me." Number two: "Oh, good idea, boss." Number three: "It was like that when I got here."' (Homer)

♦ Read Galatians 3:1–14. Why did Paul accuse the Galatians of being foolish? How does faith release us from self-justification?

♦ Read Philippians 3:1–11. Why did Paul once think he was beyond reproach spiritually? What changed his mind?

Implications

'You know, Moe, my mom once said something that really stuck with me. She said, "Homer, you're a big disappointment," and, God bless her soul, she was really onto something.' (Homer)

Choose one or more of the following questions.

♦   It could be argued that Homer's role as provider is undermined by his weaknesses. In what ways do our weaknesses undermine our roles or vocations in life?

♦   Who are you responsible for? How are you fulfilling this role? Could you do more?

♦   Are you 'big-hearted' to those around you? How is this seen?

♦   Where is the line between enjoying food and being a glutton? How close to it are you?

♦   What in your personality or background tempts you to think you are good enough for God? How is this reflected in your actions?

Prayer

Spend some time praying through these issues.

Background Reading

You will find links to some background reading on the Connect Bible Studies website: www.connectbiblestudies.com/uk/catalogue/0011/background.htm

Discuss

Discuss this study in the online discussion forums at www.connectbiblestudies.com/discuss

Members' Sheet: Part One — Homer

Summary

Homer J Simpson is the 'father-figure' in the Simpson household. He spends his days working as a safety inspector at Springfield Nuclear Power Plant where his laziness is all too visible. However, when a situation develops at the plant he manages to save it from meltdown — admittedly by guesswork.

Homer's hobbies include eating doughnuts and other fatty foods, sitting in Moe's Tavern drinking Duff beer, ten-pin bowling and baiting Ned Flanders (the Christian next door). Despite his obsession with all things culinary, Homer is a man who cares deeply for his family. His devotion to Marge is unquestionable — he even resists the temptation to have an affair with lovely Country and Western singer Lurleen Lumpkin. His love for his children — though not always clearly expressed — is evident. He is prepared to pursue various schemes to provide for their needs and wants. He tries to give them good advice when it is necessary.

Catchphrases that Homer uses include 'D'oh!' when he is upset (frequently) and 'Mmm ...' when he is tempted (even more frequently!). He has a mild disregard for the law — for a brief time he was the 'Beer Baron', producing illegal liquor during Springfield's prohibition. Homer's character underpins the whole family, and he is arguably the most important personality in the whole show.

Key Issue

Bible Study notes

Implications

Prayer

Discuss this with others on the Connect Bible Studies website: www.connectbiblestudies.com

connect

linking the Word to the world

The Simpsons

Matt Groening (20th Century Fox)

Part Two: Marge

*'The only thing I'm high on is love. Love for my son and daughters.
Yes, a little LSD is all I need.'*
Marge

Please read Using Connect Bible Studies *before leading a Bible study using this material.*

Opening Questions

Choose one of these questions.

Who is your favourite character in The Simpsons? Why?	What characteristics make a good mother?
In what ways are you — or your mother — like Marge?	Do you think only some colours are acceptable for hair dyeing? Why?

Summary

Marge the matriarch — there is no aspect of motherhood that she does not encounter. She is known for being level-headed not only at home, but also throughout the community. When Reverend Lovejoy loses his vision for listening to his parishioners' problems, Marge steps into the breach and becomes the Listen Lady. Rarely does Marge come across something in life that she cannot handle — even within her own peculiar family. She treats her three children— Bart, Lisa and baby Maggie — equally and doesn't let them get away with too much.

Her husband, Homer, struggles to put the rest of his family before his own appetites; for Marge it's second nature. But on her birthday it all becomes too much when Homer gives her a bowling ball inscribed with his own name. Marge defiantly takes up bowling and meets another man who is ready and willing to meet her needs. This spell of recklessness is soon abandoned and Marge returns to her life as household guru.

Although she cannot be present during every waking moment of her wayward family, Marge does her best to make sure they have some standing in the community. She is particularly keen for them to attend church — or at least for them to be seen going to church whether or not they receive anything from the experience. She is concerned that the family will be accepted by others — but on their own terms. After all, they are just another 'normal' family.

Key Issue: Marge — mother extraordinaire

They may not have blue hair, but how many mothers can identify with Marge and her brave attempts to hold her family together? She has a loving but lazy husband, a rebellious son, a conscientious daughter and an ever-present baby to look after. Her family seem bent on thinking up new schemes to sabotage her attempts to create a happy family life. Surely many mothers will appreciate her struggles. Marge generally tries to meet everybody's needs in a responsible way — how important is this within the Bible? What does it say about putting others first? One of Marge's aims for a respectable family lifestyle is that they should go to church. Does this make them holy? What does the Bible say about Marge's approach to life?

Bible Study

Choose one question from each section.

1.   Role — look after everyone

'Chauffeur, seamstress, curator of large mammals ...' (Marge reading out her résumé, written by Lisa)

♦   Read Exodus 18:1–27. What was Moses' motivation for judging the people? Why did Jethro challenge Moses? How did Jethro find a better way?

♦   Read Luke 10:38–42. Why did Jesus take issue with Martha's attitude? What did Mary get right?

2.   Strength — responsible

'Dear Purveyors of senseless violence: I know this may sound silly at first, but I believe that the cartoons you show to our children are influencing their behaviour in a negative way. Please try to tone down the psychotic violence in your otherwise fine programming. Yours truly, Marge Simpson.' (Marge)

♦   Read Esther 3:8, 9; 4:1–16; 7:1–4; 8:1–10. How did Mordecai's view on Esther's position challenge her? What did taking responsibility cost her?

♦   Read Luke 1:26–38. How did Mary's response to the angel change during their encounter? Why did Mary accept her new responsibility?

3.   Weakness — longing for respectability

'It doesn't matter how you feel inside, you know. It's what shows up on the surface that counts. Take all your bad feelings and push them down, all the way down, past your knees, until you're almost walking on them. And then you'll fit in, and you'll be invited to parties, and boys will like you ... and happiness will follow.' (Marge)

♦   Read Mark 12:38–44. What motivated the Pharisees? What does Jesus see as important?

♦   Read Revelation 3:1–6. What was wrong with the reputation of the church in Sardis? Why is Jesus' solution appropriate?

4.   Spiritual outlook — putting others first

'Don't thank me — thank Marge Simpson. She taught me that there's more to being a minister than not caring about people.' (Reverend Lovejoy)

♦   Read Numbers 16:41-50. What was so remarkable about Moses and Aaron putting others first? What was the result?

   Leaders: Prior to this event, Korah, Dathan and Abiram had rebelled against Moses and Aaron. God put these people and all their families to death.

♦   Read Jude 20–25. How are we to react to those around us? Why? How does Jude balance meeting others' needs with meeting our own?

Implications

'When I found out about this, I went through a wide range of emotions. First I was nervous, then anxious, then wary, then apprehensive, then ... kind of sleepy, then worried, and then concerned. But now I realize that being a spaceman is something you have to do.' (Marge to Homer)

Choose one or more of the following questions.

♦ Is it true that having lots of things to do makes us feel significant and needed? Is this good or bad and how can we learn to 'be' as much as 'do'?

♦ If you are involved in church leadership, are you doing too much? How can you share the burden with other people?

♦ How does our ultimate accountability to God affect our attitude to everyday responsibilities?

♦ How do you react to the requests God makes of us?

♦ Are you motivated to do things at church by what others may think of you? How can you change this?

♦ In what ways do you value your respectability in the eyes of others more than how God views your life? What can you do about this?

♦ Can putting others first ever go too far?

♦ How would you share the Gospel with someone like Marge?

Prayer

Spend some time praying through these issues.

Background Reading

You will find links to some background reading on the Connect Bible Studies website: www.connectbiblestudies.com/uk/catalogue/0011/background.htm

Discuss

Discuss this study in the online discussion forums at www.connectbiblestudies.com/discuss

Members' Sheet: Part Two — Marge

Summary

Marge the matriarch — there is no aspect of motherhood that she does not encounter. She is known for being level-headed not only at home, but also throughout the community. When Reverend Lovejoy loses his vision for listening to his parishioners' problems, Marge steps into the breach and becomes the Listen Lady. Rarely does Marge come across something in life that she cannot handle — even within her own peculiar family. She treats her three children— Bart, Lisa and baby Maggie — equally and doesn't let them get away with too much.

Her husband, Homer, struggles to put the rest of his family before his own appetites; for Marge it's second nature. But on her birthday it all becomes too much when Homer gives her a bowling ball inscribed with his own name. Marge defiantly takes up bowling and meets another man who is ready and willing to meet her needs. This spell of recklessness is soon abandoned and Marge returns to her life as household guru.

Although she cannot be present during every waking moment of her wayward family, Marge does her best to make sure they have some standing in the community. She is particularly keen for them to attend church — or at least for them to be seen going to church whether or not they receive anything from the experience. She is concerned that the family will be accepted by others — but on their own terms. After all, they are just another 'normal' family.

Key Issue

Bible Study notes

Implications

Prayer

Discuss this with others on the Connect Bible Studies website: www.connectbiblestudies.com

www.connectbiblestudies.com

connect
linking the Word to the world

The Simpsons

Matt Groening (20th Century Fox)

Part Three: Bart

'I'm Bart Simpson, who the hell are you?'
Bart to the Devil

Please read Using Connect Bible Studies *before leading a Bible study using this material.*

Opening Questions

Choose one of these questions.

How true to life is the character of Bart?	Is rebellion ever a good thing? Why?
How would you cope if Bart was your brother?	Would you be friends with Bart? Why or why not?

Summary

Bart Simpson, rebel of the Simpson household, makes life simultaneously wild and wonderful for those around him. An underachiever at school, he is the prime suspect for any crime or misdemeanour and a constant torment to Principal Skinner.

To some, Bart is also an icon. He can always be relied upon to make a joke out of a situation. He once cheated on an intelligence test and was mistaken for a child genius. In his brief life Bart has vandalised the statue of Springfield's founder in an attempt to win the approval of a group of older children, led a rag-tag army in battle against school bully Nelson Muntz, and was at the centre of a rebellion at Camp Krusty after it failed to meet the promised standards.

One of Bart's favourite pranks is to make hoax calls to Moe's Tavern which are designed to trick Moe into saying something rude. Bart is fiercely pro-Springfield and has little tolerance for the neighbouring rival town of Shelbyville. Bart brings life and vitality to the family.

Without him, the Simpsons would be a more mundane unit. One of his good points is that he loves his family deeply — and occasionally reveals this to them.

Key Issue: Bart — the boy

Fun-loving, mischievous, rebellious — Bart has a reputation which many boys would envy. He does his own thing on all possible occasions, and shows little respect for authority. He is not afraid of creating trouble, yet manages to endear himself to us with his charm, love of fun and self-aware moments of insecurity. Does the Bible condemn his cavalier approach to living? What does it say about rebellion and the way he tries to cheat his way through life? How far can a provocative approach go before it becomes damaging?

Bible Study

Choose one question from each section.

1. Role — rebel

'Man, I wish I was an adult so I could break the rules.' (Bart)

- ◆ Read Proverbs 20:9–11. How extensive and intensive is human rebellion? How is this seen?

- ◆ Read 2 Timothy 3:1–9. What does human rebellion look like? What are the roots of it?

   Leaders: Jannes and Jambres are the traditional names for Pharaoh's magicians at the time of Moses.

2. Strength — enjoying life

'A boy without mischief is like a bowling ball with a liquid centre.' (Homer)

- ◆ Read Psalm 126. What was the source of the author's joy? How was it expressed?

   Leaders: This Psalm was probably composed after return from exile in Babylon. It would have been sung in public upon approach to the temple in Jerusalem.

- ◆ Read Romans 12:14–16. What principles are laid down for interaction with people? How will this help preserve 'harmony'?

3. Weakness — provocative

'Wow, Mom, I never pictured you as any kind of authority figure before.' (Bart)

- ◆ Read Proverbs 26:18, 19; 27:3; Ecclesiastes 7:9. What is the danger in provocation — both for those who are being provoked and for those doing the provoking? Why is provocation a heavy burden?

- ◆ Read Matthew 12:1–14. How do the Pharisees and Jesus provoke each other? Is there any difference between them?

4. Spiritual outlook — cheat

'Dear God, we paid for all this stuff ourselves, so thanks for nothing.' (Bart)

- ◆ Read Malachi 1:6–14. What did the priests' shortcuts reveal about their attitude to God? Why does God respond to this in the way described?

  Leaders: Malachi is the last book chronologically in the Old Testament. Israel had returned from exile and rebuilt the temple, yet they were still falling short of what God expected from them.

- ◆ Read Philippians 3:12–16. Does Paul see any place in the Christian life for spiritual shortcuts? What is Paul's advice for day-to-day spirituality?

  Leaders: Paul has been talking about the value of knowing Christ and a desire to know Him more.

Implications

'I didn't do it. No one saw me do it. No one can prove anything.' (Bart)

Choose one or more of the following questions.

◆ Are you rebelling against God in some way? What can you do about it?

◆ Is there enough fun in your life? Do you think God wants you to have fun?

◆ Can you think of any situations where provoking someone would be the right thing to do? What might you stand to gain or lose?

◆ Are you easily provoked or subjected to painful teasing? How can you let God into those fragile areas which make you vulnerable?

◆ What spiritual shortcuts have you tried? What happened?

◆ What would you say to someone who asked your advice on dealing with a son like Bart?

Prayer

Spend some time praying through these issues.

Background Reading

You will find links to some background reading on the Connect Bible Studies website:
www.connectbiblestudies.com/uk/catalogue/0011/background.htm

Discuss

Discuss this study in the online discussion forums at www.connectbiblestudies.com/discuss

Members' Sheet: Part Three — Bart

Summary

Bart Simpson, rebel of the Simpson household, makes life simultaneously wild and wonderful for those around him. An underachiever at school, he is the prime suspect for any crime or misdemeanour and a constant torment to Principal Skinner.

To some, Bart is also an icon. He can always be relied upon to make a joke out of a situation. He once cheated on an intelligence test and was mistaken for a child genius. In his brief life Bart has vandalised the statue of Springfield's founder in an attempt to win the approval of a group of older children, led a rag-tag army in battle against school bully Nelson Muntz, and was at the centre of a rebellion at Camp Krusty after it failed to meet the promised standards.

One of Bart's favourite pranks is to make hoax calls to Moe's Tavern which are designed to trick Moe into saying something rude. Bart is fiercely pro-Springfield and has little tolerance for the neighbouring rival town of Shelbyville. Bart brings life and vitality to the family. Without him, the Simpsons would be a more mundane unit. One of his good points is that he loves his family deeply — and occasionally reveals this to them.

Key Issue

Bible Study notes

Implications

Prayer

Discuss this with others on the Connect Bible Studies website: www.connectbiblestudies.com

connect

linking the Word to the world

The Simpsons

Matt Groening (20th Century Fox)

Part Four: Lisa

'A man who envies our family is a man who needs help.'
(Lisa)

Please read Using Connect Bible Studies *before leading a Bible study using this material.*

Opening Questions

Choose one of these questions.

Do you sympathise with Lisa? Why or why not?	Would you like Lisa as a friend? Why or why not?
Why does Lisa enjoy school so much?	Is perfectionism a good or a bad thing? Why?

Summary

Lisa is a remarkably likeable swot. Surprisingly intelligent, she is determined to prove that she can get good grades, in spite of having an older brother whose appalling reputation always goes before her. Failure is not an option for Lisa and she has a tendency to strive after perfection in everything. When a brighter girl moves into Springfield, Lisa's whole sense of identity is threatened. Even when she seems to be failing at sport, she finds something that she can do well — being a goalkeeper in ice hockey. Unfortunately, she ends up battling against Bart in a competition. However, the experience turns into a valuable lesson in humility when the pair decide to put down their sticks and call it a draw.

More than just a brain, Lisa performs the role of moral crusader in the family unit. Sometimes she is the only person to comment when Homer dreams up another dubious scheme for getting the family out of its latest scrape.

Lisa's intellectual nature leads her to an appreciation of the finer things in life. She loves jazz music and can often be heard around the neighbourhood playing her saxophone — which, of course, she does brilliantly. She is passionate about being fair and is the driving force behind the campaign to save the snakes of Springfield from being beaten to death on Whacking Day.

Key Issue: Lisa — conscientious daughter

Love her or hate her, Lisa seems to be the opposite in character to her brother Bart. Unlike him, she is hard-working, conscientious and perfectionist in her approach to life. Her sense of right and wrong is very strong, and she applies this to her spiritual outlook as well. She often tries to influence her family to do what she sees as the right thing. This all sounds good, but what does the Bible say? Would it support her perfectionism and longing for order in life and religion? Does the Bible give guidelines about how hard we should work, and what we should do if we think others have gone off the rails?

Bible Study

Choose one question from each section.

1. Role — moral conscience

'I never realized before, but some Itchy & Scratchy cartoons send the message that violence against animals is funny.' (Lisa)

- ◆ Read 1 Kings 21:1–29. Why did Ahab need someone else to be his moral conscience? How did Elijah fulfil this role? What was Ahab's response?

- ◆ Read Mark 6:7, 12–29. Why did Herod need someone else to be his moral conscience? How did John fulfil this role? What was Herod's response?

2. Strength — hard working

'Grades are all I have.' (Lisa)

- ◆ Read Colossians 3:22–4:1. What are the motivations for working hard? What are the characteristics of hard work?

  Leaders: This initially referred to slaves and masters in the literal sense. However, the principles can be applied to today — in our work situations, for example.

- ◆ Read 2 Peter 1:3–11. What does Peter say we should work hard at? What's the balance between our work and God's work in us?

3. Weakness — perfectionist

'Relax? I can't relax. Nor can I yield, relent, or ... Only two synonyms? Oh! ... I'm losing my perspicacity!' (Lisa)

♦ Read Matthew 19:16–26. Why did Jesus tell the man to do something that wasn't required by the Jewish law? What are the implications of Jesus' response to the disciples' question in verse 25?

Leaders: There is no evidence of there ever being a gate called The Eye of the Needle in the Jerusalem wall through which a camel could only pass on its knees and without baggage — it's a Christian myth. The point of Jesus' image of a camel being unable to go through the eye of a needle is not that it is hard but that it is impossible (as is made clear in verse 26) — it's a joke.

♦ Read James 3:1–12. Is perfection possible? How does James illustrate his answer?

4. Spiritual outlook — wants everything in order

'I heard you last night, Bart. You prayed for this. Now your prayers have been answered ... and you owe him big.' (Lisa)

♦ Read 1 Corinthians 14:26–40. Why is orderly worship necessary? How does Paul expand this principle?

Leaders: In the culture Paul was addressing, women were downtrodden and deemed inferior. Through the Gospel, women had significant freedom. Paul is asking that women should not disrupt services by misusing their new freedom and asking numerous questions. It is Paul's belief that women should have the opportunity to learn that is so shocking here, not his instruction for women to be quiet in church. This was revolutionary in Corinthian culture.

♦ Read Hebrews 10:1-25. The Jewish sacrificial system was extremely ordered. Why does the writer say that it was not the 'be all and end all' in a relationship with God? How does Jesus supercede the system?

Implications

'I don't get it. Straight 'A's, perfect attendance, Bathroom Timer ... I should be the most popular girl in school.' (Lisa)

Choose one or more of the following questions.

- How do we know if, when and how it is appropriate to talk to others if they are heading for trouble?

- Are there areas in our lives where we have squashed the voice of conscience? Is now the time to listen to it?

- Do you think you work too hard or not hard enough? Would others around you agree?

- Does Jesus' command, 'Be perfect, therefore, as your heavenly Father is perfect,' (Matthew 5:48) mean we should be perfectionist?

- What is the difference between helpful order and restrictive rules in our spiritual and church lives? What does God want?

Prayer

Spend some time praying through these issues.

Background Reading

You will find links to some background reading on the Connect Bible Studies website: www.connectbiblestudies.com/uk/catalogue/0011/background.htm

Discuss

Discuss this study in the online discussion forums at www.connectbiblestudies.com/discuss

Members' Sheet: Part Four — Lisa

Summary

Lisa is a remarkably likeable swot. Surprisingly intelligent, she is determined to prove that she can get good grades, in spite of having an older brother whose appalling reputation always goes before her. Failure is not an option for Lisa and she has a tendency to strive after perfection in everything. When a brighter girl moves into Springfield, Lisa's whole sense of identity is threatened. Even when she seems to be failing at sport, she finds something that she can do well — being a goalkeeper in ice hockey. Unfortunately, she ends up battling against Bart in a competition. However, the experience turns into a valuable lesson in humility when the pair decide to put down their sticks and call it a draw.

More than just a brain, Lisa performs the role of moral crusader in the family unit. Sometimes she is the only person to comment when Homer dreams up another dubious scheme for getting the family out of its latest scrape.

Lisa's intellectual nature leads her to an appreciation of the finer things in life. She loves jazz music and can often be heard around the neighbourhood playing her saxophone — which, of course, she does brilliantly. She is passionate about being fair and is the driving force behind the campaign to save the snakes of Springfield from being beaten to death on Whacking Day.

Key Issue

Bible Study notes

Implications

Prayer